This is the only known colour photograph of Sir Stenson Cooke, who was appointed Secretary of the Automobile Association in August 1905, shortly after the AA's foundation, at the age of thirty-one. From a solicitor's borrowed room at 18 Fleet Street, London, with a 'lady typewriter', ninety members and a small bank balance, he directed the AA into becoming the world's largest motoring organisation. Knowing nothing of motoring, then in its infancy, he was able to apply a fresh and unbiased mind to the problems of 'automobilism', as motoring was then called. It was Cooke who selected the Latin word 'Fanum' (temple) for the AA's telegraphic address, as he saw the AA as 'the temple of motoring'. Cooke was an ardent fencer, a member of the British fencing team at the Olympic Games of 1912, and represented Great Britain on a number of occasions. He was a finalist in the British Amateur Championship of 1923. He served as a Captain in the Rifle Brigade before the First World War and in 1914 led a contingent of AA patrols to enlist in the 8th (Cyclist) Battalion of the Essex Regiment. He was promoted to Major and served as Controller of Supplies at the Ministry of National Service. He was decorated by many governments and knighted in 1933 for his services to motoring and tourism. His book 'This Motoring' (seen in the photograph above), relating the story of the AA, was published in 1930 and ran to eighteen editions. Cooke also wrote short stories and a book on travel. After thirty-seven years of service, Sir Stenson Cooke died in office at Guildford (the AA's wartime headquarters) in November 1942 at the age of sixty-eight. He is buried at Hampstead Cemetery, Fortune Green Road, although the headstone makes no mention of his knighthood or connection with the AA.

The AA:
History, Badges and Memorabilia

Michael Passmore

A Shire book

Published in 2003 by Shire Publications Ltd,
Cromwell House, Church Street, Princes Risborough,
Buckinghamshire HP27 9AA, UK.
(Website: www.shirebooks.co.uk)

British Library Cataloguing in Publication Data:
Passmore, Michael
The AA: history, badges and memorabilia.
– (Shire album; 414)
1. Automobile Association – History
2. Automobile Association – Insignia
3. Automobile Association – Collectables
I. Title 629.2'83'060941
ISBN 0 7478 0552 0

Editorial Consultant: Michael E. Ware, former Director of the National Motor Museum, Beaulieu.

Cover: *A very rare colour photograph of patrols in training at the AA National Training College,
Widmerpool, Nottinghamshire, in the 1950s.*
Back cover: *A montage of AA badges.*

ACKNOWLEDGEMENTS

Thanks are due to The Automobile Association for permission to use the photographs shown
in this book, which are all either from the AA Archive or have been specially commissioned.

Printed in Malta by Gutenberg Press Limited, Gudja Road,
Tarxien PLA19, Malta

Contents

A short history of
The Automobile Association

At the start of the twentieth century, motor cars were considered dangerous nuisances, creating clouds of dust on unmade roads and frightening the population. The police reacted by setting up speed traps hiding behind hedges and timing motorists over a set distance. But often the distances were short of the measured furlong or the hand-held stopwatches were inaccurate, started too late or stopped too soon. The main motor roads were in the south of England, and Captain Mowbray Sant of the Surrey police set in place a trapping mania that soon was raising hundreds of pounds in speeding fines. The speed limit after 1st January 1904 was 20 mph (32 km/h), and cars could easily do 30 mph (48 km/h) and more on open roads with no traffic at all on them.

Although the Royal Automobile Club had been formed earlier than the AA (in 1897), the RAC was much more interested in the development of the motor car itself, and consequently promoted speed trials, races, hill-climbs and other motor-sport activities. At that time the RAC did not provide any on-the-road services to motorists itself, but through a subsidiary organisation, the Motor Union. However, the MU initially did nothing to counter trapping.

So in 1905 a group of fewer than twenty motoring enthusiasts met at the Trocadero Restaurant, in Leicester Square, London, to consider ways

One of the very first AA cycle scouts of 1905, John Drew is pictured here in 1910 wearing a warning disc. He later became a Superintendent and was in charge of the AA team dealing with car parking at Wimbledon. When he died in 1936 he was given a full AA funeral.

4

to combat police persecution. They wanted a protective organisation to counter this anti-car activity – and so they formed what soon became called the Automobile Association. They decided to set up a fleet of cycle scouts to patrol the main motor roads and warn members of any police traps ahead. Some scouts were recruited from Fleet Street newsboys, who could easily cycle to the roads of Surrey and who worked for the AA only at weekends. Eventually one of them was arrested for obstructing the police in their duty, but the AA Secretary, Stenson Cooke, hit on a simple solution. The scouts, who had previously saluted members as a matter of courtesy, would no longer salute if there was a trap – and so they could not be prosecuted for doing nothing!

Stenson Cooke is considered by many to be the founding father of the AA, but this is not so. He was the chief architect and a man of ideas, but he was appointed after the AA was formed, as a paid official. He was not a motorist – as far as is known he never drove a car in his life – but under his leadership the AA grew into the United Kingdom's foremost motoring organisation, a position it still holds today. One of Cooke's early bright ideas was to transport a battalion of guardsmen from London to Hastings in 1909, using members' cars, to show how useful the motor car could be

The Guards to Hastings run in March 1909. It snowed and the guardsmen, travelling in open cars, would have been bitterly cold, despite wearing greatcoats.

The first AA road sign, 1906. It stood on the Sutton to Reigate road at Banstead Downs, Surrey.

– thus the AA can claim to have invented the concept of motorised infantry. The run was widely reported in the press, particularly in Germany.

As more and more cars came on to the roads, mainly owned by wealthy and 'respectable' people, the era of the speed trap came to an end and the AA started to concentrate on providing service to motorists. The subscription fee had been set at 2 guineas (£2 2s – £2.10), the equivalent of around two weeks' average wages. This comparatively high initial fee was maintained for years, and in the days of low inflation enabled the AA to provide wide-ranging services from the outset. The first services to be introduced were handwritten route maps, free legal defence and the erection of location signs and warning signs, the first being a 'slow' sign put up in 1906. The AA was the only national signposting authority until the 1930s, when the government gave the responsibility to local authorities. The AA published its first handbook, listing hotels and garage agents, in 1908.

Then in 1910 the Secretary of the Motor Union was appointed to a government post, and the Chairman of the AA resigned because of ill health. The MU had separated from the RAC in 1907 because of the MU's increasing co-operation with the AA on road matters, and so at the end of 1910 the two organisations combined, 8527 MU members joining 19,513 AA members. The President of the combined AA&MU (as it was officially known) was the fifth Earl of Lonsdale, known as the 'Yellow Earl' from the

6

colour of his racing livery. It is often erroneously thought that this is the origin of the AA house colours yellow and black, but in fact they had been in use for some years previously and the choice of colours seems to have been arbitrary. The amalgamation gave rise to a new winged badge, formed by the outline and wings of the MU badge surrounding the crossed 'A's of the AA. This badge was to last for fifty-five years and be recognised the world over.

From 1911 sentry-box-style telephone boxes started to be put up at important crossroads, from where members could ring for assistance or make local calls free of charge. Petrol, oil and water were also stored in the box, which was a base for the patrol. The patrol could also be contacted by telephone from the AA headquarters if he was needed to help a motorist not on his cycle beat.

By 1914 the membership had grown to 83,000 out of 132,000 cars registered. Military-style uniforms had been introduced in 1911 and hotels

The first-pattern AA box. Outside stands an AA patrol in the first full uniform.

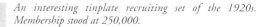

An interesting tinplate recruiting set of the 1920s. Membership stood at 250,000.

had been graded by the now famous star system from 1912. Tradition has it that Stenson Cooke thought up the scheme, copying the idea from the way brandy was graded – one star for the worst, five stars for the best. More branch offices had been opened throughout the United Kingdom and the AA headquarters had moved from its small office in Fleet Street to a building in Leicester Square.

When war was declared in August 1914, Secretary Stenson Cooke led 120 AA patrols with their bicycles down the Embankment to Liverpool Street Station, London, where they entrained for enlistment in the 8th (Cyclist) Battalion of the Essex Regiment. Through the AA, members offered their cars for service with the War Office, their chauffeurs being formed into the AA Voluntary Service Corps. The AA also provided a fleet of ambulances for service at the front, with AA badges as well as red crosses painted on their sides.

After the end of the First World War, the AA expanded enormously – it had 100,000 members in 1920 and 250,000 members by 1925 out of 580,000 cars registered. Mass-produced cars such as Fords and Austins brought motoring to many more people, and the AA's services grew accordingly. Motorcycle combinations were introduced from 1919 (although inspectors had ridden solos from 1912 and some patrols were still on cycles up to 1939). Printed route maps and guidebooks were published, AA signs were seen everywhere and members were issued with their own keys to the increasing number of telephone boxes. It was the AA which opened the first roadside petrol filling station (at Aldermaston, Berkshire, in 1920) and another ten were built before the petrol companies finally realised what a good idea they were and opened their own. The AA then withdrew, as their involvement had not been for commercial reasons but just to show the way forward. The first reflective roadside

A typical 1920s Road Service Outfit, showing the kit carried in the box. A brown overall and foul-weather clothing were also carried. Note the acetylene-powered lights.

The first roadside filling station, at Aldermaston in Berkshire. Other AA stations had canopies over the filling area.

AA Headquarters, Fanum House, London. On the left Leicester Square can be seen; on the right is Whitcombe Street. The building on the right was the first AA office in Whitcombe Street; later the one on the left was taken over as well, then the building behind (shown being rebuilt). Eventually the other two were demolished and rebuilt in the same style, and by 1959 the rest of the site had also been acquired.

Apart from handbooks, the AA published a huge range of touring and information guides. A selection of just a few leaflets, mainly pre-war.

warning signs were put up in 1919, by the AA. These had a number of small glass reflectors (known as 'bull's-eyes') mounted in them, which reflected light when a headlight caught them. (Percy Shaw of Halifax invented 'cat's-eyes', first installed at Market Harborough, Leicestershire, in 1934.) In 1924 the AA started work on its new headquarters building, Fanum House in Leicester Square, London. The building was extended progressively, although it was not until 1959 that the building occupied the whole of the island site.

Private flying became increasingly popular, and so in 1928 an AA Aviation Section was formed, issuing flying maps and maps of landing grounds in the United Kingdom, updated by patrols in the area. The record-breaking flyers Amy Johnson and Jim Mollinson flew with AA maps. A twelve-man Aviation Squad supplied AA-uniformed mechanics at the major air shows and meetings. In 1931 an AA-operated radio station

The Aviation Squad, 1929. The men had all previously served in the RAF. The overalls were yellow, with the very early wearing of black berets, then normally sported flat on the head, not to one side.

A wartime AA patrol. He wears an AA-badged steel helmet and the motorcycle is camouflaged.

was built at Heston aerodrome in Middlesex (now the site of the westbound services on the M4), which broadcast weather information to pilots. (Heston was the aerodrome to which Neville Chamberlain flew back after the 1938 Munich Agreement, with his famous 'Peace for our time' piece of paper.)

The 1930s (with 400,000 AA members in 1930 and just over one million cars registered) were the golden years of motoring, with few cars on the roads – only one family in fifty had one, but nearly half of them were AA members. Stenson Cooke published his book *This Motoring* to celebrate the first twenty-five years of the AA (a copy was sent to every AA member until September 1939, by which time membership stood at 725,000) and in 1933 he was knighted for his services to motoring. New motorcycles and more telephone boxes were brought into use. Thousands more AA road signs were put up.

AA patrols had volunteered for service in the Territorial Army, training as military policemen, and for this reason British troops on the beaches of Dunkirk in 1940 were marshalled there by military police who were often former AA patrols. Those patrols remaining in Britain were issued with AA-badged steel helmets and had their motorcycles sprayed in camouflage colours. The AA Aviation Section was taken over by the Air Ministry and the AA routes department issued maps to United States servicemen in Britain.

With Britain making a slow recovery after the Second World War, rationing remained in force, often at lower than wartime levels. At one point petrol was entirely withdrawn for private motoring, but after a joint petition from the AA and RAC a small allowance was introduced. Rationing was ended only in 1950. In 1947 the AA took delivery of its one-thousandth BSA motorcycle. A radio service was launched in London in 1949 and was gradually extended to the rest of the country, allowing

The AA's first Land Rover outside the AA garage at Bayham Street, Camden Town, London. (The building still stands – and the Land Rover still exists.)

patrols to be sent direct to breakdowns without having to cover set beats. The same year the AA bought its first Land Rover, one of the first thousand built. (This vehicle was sold out of service in 1953 but was rediscovered in 1994, bought back and restored. It is currently on display at Milestones Museum in Basingstoke, Hampshire, together with the rest of the AA's historic collection.) The millionth AA member was enrolled in 1950, when there were 2.25 million cars registered.

By the time of the AA's Golden Jubilee in 1955, new open-neck uniforms had been brought into use, and then crash helmets. The motorcycles were fitted with

Below: *The new uniform of 1947. The patrol rides an M20 BSA with coffin-shaped box and is wearing a white cap cover for the summer. The chain on his tunic connects to an AA-marked whistle in his pocket.*

Above: *The London Pilot Service was set up in 1951 to provide a (female) driver for members unfamiliar with London. They would be met at an outer Underground station and then driven to their destination. Uniforms for these women were the same as for uniformed receptionists at mobile offices and the like, except for a specialist arm badge with the title 'Pilot Service' – not to be confused with 'Air Service', worn by the AA's flying staff! The Pilot Service uniforms were at first copied from the wartime ATS but were replaced by the type seen here in the 1960s.*

A line-up of AA vehicles, as well as a mobile office and telephone box, in the early 1960s. Note the flag.

fibreglass windshields and aerodynamically styled sidecar boxes. All the pre-war telephone boxes were replaced with a new pattern. In their heyday there were nearly one thousand boxes in service – in 2000 only twenty-two remained. The aviation section was reformed to become mainly an air-ambulance service, repatriating AA members who had suffered accident or illness in Europe. The most famous aircraft operated was a De Havilland Rapide, G-AHKV, also used for traffic spotting and to drop supplies to snowbound villages in Scotland. Membership reached two million in 1958.

By the middle of the 1960s, traffic had increased fourfold from pre-war days and the motorcycle combination simply could not cope, not to mention the difficulty of riding one in freezing rain. The famous AA salute had been abolished for patrols on the move in 1961 on safety grounds, as it was simply impractical, if not dangerous, with so many members on the road. Minivans became the first standard-issue four-wheel patrol fleet vehicle from 1965. The concept of the AA man on his yellow motorcycle had been an enduring one, starting from 1920, but the last one was withdrawn from service

AA Pilot Bill Lewis. A former RAF Mosquito pilot, with the moustache to prove it, Bill Lewis piloted all the AA's prop-driven aircraft, including the De Havilland Rapide seen behind him here. With him is another AA pilot, Don Whitehead. Note the car badge on the plane's nose.

Minivans being driven from the Austin factory. This was the first delivery but later it was not an unusual sight, as Road Service Outfits and vans were normally purchased in batches. The Minivan appeared in both winged-badge and square-logo liveries.

in 1968. This coincided with the introduction in 1967 of the new square logo, reflecting the AA's move into a more modern world, and the establishment of its own insurance underwriting service (it had been selling other companies' policies since 1907). After the collapse of Vehicle & General in 1971, AA members who were left without cover queued for hours to get AA insurance – the clerks were working so hard they had to throw completed forms and money into dustbins used as collection points! Membership reached 3 million in 1963 (out of 7.3 million cars registered) and 4 million in 1969, despite the subscription fee rising for the first time since 1905, when it increased from 2 guineas (£2 2s – £2.10) to 3 guineas (£3 3s – £3.15) in 1965.

Alexander Durie, the first chief executive to be appointed from outside

A Bedford J3 transporter. This was the first Relay recovery vehicle – one has been preserved in the AA's historic collection.

The first-pattern AA telephone pedestal. It was known as the 'ice-cream cone' or 'wineglass' type. A later one was the 'sardine can' pattern. The 1990s column type was called the 'pencil'.

the AA (in 1965), brought in more changes in the 1970s: new uniforms less military in style, the introduction of Relay (recovery for cars that could not be repaired on the road), Roadwatch (traffic information broadcasts), centralisation, computerisation, commercialisation, telephone pedestals in place of the boxes, and the move of the AA headquarters from London to Basingstoke. More changes came in the 1980s: different types of specialist vehicles and a variety of vans for the patrol service, plastic 'credit card' type membership certificates, and increased lobbying of Parliament, such as support for the compulsory wearing of seat belts. There were six million members recorded in 1987 and seven million in 1988, the year the first female patrol was recruited.

In 1992 the AA launched its own driving school. Membership reached 8 million in 1994, and the same year the headquarters moved from Fanum House to Norfolk House, still in Basingstoke. As more members and customers contacted the AA by telephone, it was decided to close the network of high-street AA shops and, to improve the breakdown service further, to set up three major deployment operations supercentres in place of the numerous smaller ones.

During the 1990s the AA presented itself as the 'Fourth Emergency Service' to its members, after the police, ambulance and fire brigade. Some – particularly coastguards – might question this, but AA patrols have rescued people from fires, crashes and floods. Forty-seven AA patrols have been killed in the course of their duties assisting the public.

In September 1999, when membership was almost 10 million, the AA was sold to Centrica, the leading supplier of energy and services to homes in Great Britain, for £1.1 billion. The era of the mutual AA came to a close, but the name and badge are still on Britain's roads, still providing service to motorists. The AA is regarded with respect and indeed affection by the general public – in 1998/9 the BBC broadcast a twelve-episode AA-based television comedy series called *The Last Salute*.

New products and services are frequently introduced. In 2001 the AA bought Halfords Garages and re-branded them as AA Service Centres, offering members discounts on car repairs and maintenance services. In 2002 the AA announced that its roadside telephone boxes would be taken out of service because of the high cost of their maintenance and the prevalence of mobile telephones.

The AA is the largest motor insurance intermediary in the United Kingdom and through the AA Driving School teaches 100,000 people to drive every year. It is also Britain's largest travel publisher, with more than 650 titles, including its renowned atlases and guides. The AA continues to be the leading voice of the motorist, campaigning for better roads and a better deal for Britain's 30 million drivers, and offers a widening range of services for choosing, purchasing, owning and running a car.

With more than 12 million members and 3600 patrols, the AA remains the United Kingdom's largest motoring organisation. Constantly investing in new technology is crucial to its success. Its latest patrol vehicles are fitted with route-guidance systems, ensuring that most breakdowns are attended within thirty-five minutes. Eight out of ten cars are repaired at the side of the road and, if the AA cannot mend a car there, it has specially designed vehicles equipped with modern recovery apparatus. The AA has a brand image that is second to none, a just position after a century of service to the motorist.

A montage of AA badges, used on the cover of the 1980 handbook for the AA's seventy-fifth anniversary.

AA presents. (From top) Bowls and a mug for the seventy-fifth anniversary (a large plate with the armorial bearings was also produced by Spode), silver-plated menu holder, silver bookmark, compact for female staff with twenty-five years' service (the men got a cigarette box; from 1990 all staff got badges), pre-war members' diary, Christmas greetings record sent in 1938 by Sir Stenson Cooke, and a paperweight made from marble retrieved from the entrance hall at Leicester Square when the move was made to Basingstoke.

Collecting AA memorabilia

The AA has produced a wide range of collectables, ranging from car badges and insignia to road signs and vehicles.

Apart from car badges, the earliest artefacts still around are the circular discs worn by cycle scouts, and bearing the number of the patrol. One side was white to signify 'all clear', the other red to warn of danger ahead –

A selection of membership cards, certificates, holders and modern plastic cards.

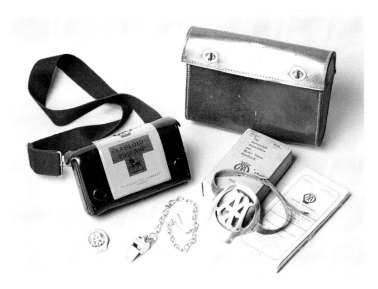

Early cycle-scout items, including first-aid kit, handlebar toolkit, brass arm badge, whistle and cap badge.

normally a police speed trap. Sometimes these cycle scouts also wore an armband on their civilian jackets with the wording 'AA Patrol'. The first uniformed patrols wore a sash over one shoulder (blue for patrols, red for inspectors), which supported a small leather first-aid pouch, and carried AA-marked whistles. In addition they wore an arm badge made of brass in the shape of an AA badge, threaded on to a leather strap worn round the arm, just above the left elbow.

Enamelled signs such as this were put up below much larger AA signs in the belief that they would provoke small boys to throw stones at the reward sign instead of damaging the more expensive one above.

£2 REWARD

WILL BE PAID FOR INFORMATION LEADING TO THE CONVICTION OF ANY PERSON OR PERSONS DAMAGING THESE SIGNS

BY ORDER

THE AUTOMOBILE ASSOCIATION & MOTOR UNION, 12 COLLEGE GREEN, DUBLIN.

Car badges

Car badges have always been and will remain the most popular area of AA memorabilia collecting. The first AA badge was issued in March 1906, nine months after the initial formation of the Association, because it was necessary to have a means of identifying members to the cycle scouts so that they could be warned about speed traps. The first prototype was shown to the Committee on 13th March 1906 and, after requesting that it be made an inch (25 mm) bigger and with a longer shank, they approved it. The first batch was made by the firm of Nash & Hull, but from December 1906 and for the next sixty years the badges were made by Walter Rowley Limited of Aston Road, Birmingham, who also made a bewildering range of fittings listed in a twenty-page catalogue.

Members were charged a hire fee of 5 shillings for a brass badge and 7 shillings for a nickel-plated one. The first one hundred were hand-cut, the design being a circle surrounding two crossed 'A's, with a fixing shank below. Badge number 1 was issued in April 1906 to the AA's first Chairman, Colonel Bosworth, and number 2 to the Vice Chairman (this badge is in the AA historic collection on display at Milestones Museum, Basingstoke). Badge numbers were impressed on the top of the badge, with Stenson Cooke's signature (and, shortly after, the word 'Secretary') stamped below. These are known as 'Stenson Cooke badges' by collectors and 'frying pan badges' by AA staff. At the end of 1906, the AA's telephone number and telegraphic address ('Fanum, London') were also included, on the reverse. A smaller motorcycle version was issued from November 1907, of which only two thousand were made, beginning with the number 10001.

First-pattern AA badges. Badge number 1 is at the top, and below it a hand-crafted example with a very long shank.

*Developing the badge.
A first-pattern AA
badge plus a Motor
Union badge equals
the winged version.*

Car badge number 1 was later taken over by Stenson Cooke and worn on his car until his death. It is currently in the possession of his granddaughter. There are a number of replicas of the first-pattern badge. One was made by the AA itself in the 1930s, and more were made by the AA in 1955 for issue to Veteran Car Club members who took part in the re-enactment of the Guards to Hastings run as part of the AA's fiftieth anniversary (stamped '1905–1955' at the bottom). Yet more were AA-made for commercial purposes (stamped with the dates 1905–1911) and others have been copied privately.

At the end of 1910 the AA merged with the Motor Union. As a result, the wings on the MU badge (a winged wheel seen head on) and the expanded surround of the stylised 'M' were carried over into a new AA badge registered on 2nd February 1911, the basic form of which lasted until 1967 (when the modern square logo was introduced). The first new badge was issued in April. The winged badge was registered as a trademark in 1914 *and is still AA copyright.* Some AA members at the time of the merger transferred the wings of their MU badge and riveted them on to an original round AA badge, but the first properly produced winged AA badge occurred some time between the numbers 27467 and 28033, these being the last unwinged and first winged badges seen so far.

In June 1911, following the merger, the AA had 31,851 members (more than half the number of cars registered), indicating that the vast majority had badges. A nickel new-style badge was available from October 1912, and a motorcycle version from 1911. A pentagonal 'light car' version was introduced in May 1914, but this category of membership was phased out in 1920. These badge numbers run from 150000 to 218999, but only thirty thousand such badges were produced.

During the First World War, for two years, special heart-shaped inserts were issued for attachment to motorcycle badges to indicate membership renewal – blue to March 1915 and red to March 1916. The system was not, however, extended.

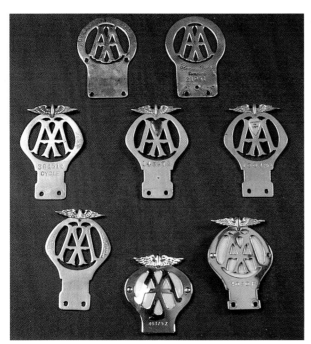

Motorcycle badges, including two with heart-shaped renewal tokens.

In 1911 an industrial vehicle badge was designed, a brass hexagon shape with a red-painted background. It may not actually have been issued until 1922, however. In the early 1930s (at around badge number V50000) it was redesigned in chrome with a basket-weave background, and it was issued in large and small versions until 1966 – the numbers are all prefixed with the letter V.

During the 1920s and 1930s the badge itself came in several variations, such as right-angle shanks, radiator- or bumper-fitting holes, large and small sizes, and with optional backing plates in yellow or sometimes black. Nickel and then chrome-plated badges became more popular in the 1920s than brass ones because of the increasing use of chrome on car bodies. The last brass badge issues recorded were the 691000–691999 series

Industrial vehicle badges. Pre-war and post-war versions, including the red-painted first issue.

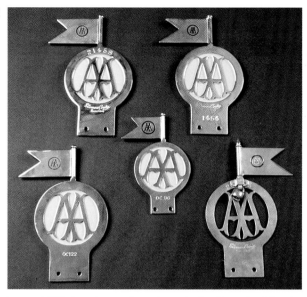

Committee members' badges, including one with detachable flag and padlock, shown bottom right.

of June to August 1931, but there exists a brass badge from the M series of 1937–47.

Committee members were issued with a special badge – the first design, but with a small flag added to the top. An example exists where the flag is removable and held in place with a tiny padlock, but normally they are brazed on. There is no pattern to whether the flags face left or right – it seems to be at the whim of whoever produced them. Until the Second World War, these Committee badges were all original first-pattern badges which had been modified – thus a Committee member of 1939 could have been issued with a badge thirty years old. New versions were issued after the war, the OC series (see below).

Badges were consecutively numbered up to 999999, which was issued in October 1930. That same year the numbers started again but prefixed 0 to only 09999, but then each 100,000 had a suffix letter A to T, which lasted until 1958. For example, 75000 was issued in 1912, 07500 was issued in 1930 (as were all 0-prefixed numbers), 75000A in 1931, 75000T in 1955. The letters M, N and P covered the wartime years. The R to Z series were issued post-war and were allocated to motorcycle badges. Unfortunately, motorcycle-badge series numbers continued after Z with A – which can cause confusion with the car-badge A series issued between June 1930 and August 1931, although of course the badge patterns are different.

Some pre-war badges have the letter R stamped on them *below* the normal number. Because the badge fee was a hire fee and not a purchase fee, badges are often marked from 1924 with the message 'Property of the Automobile Association – this badge MUST be returned when membership ceases', since possession of a badge in those days was considered proof of entitlement to service (theoretically the AA still owns all badges so marked). So when members did cease their membership, the badge was generally returned and if it was in good enough condition it was refurbished and reissued, stamped with an R to indicate that. Hire fees were 5s 0d to 1920, 7s 6d to 1945 and 10s 0d to 1967.

In 1945 the AA badge was completely redesigned. The new style incorporated a permanent yellow backing plate, the front was slightly bulged out and the legs of the 'A's merged with the surround. The first one was issued on 8th October 1945 and a smaller size was introduced for motorcycles from 1952 (the R series mentioned above).

The new badge numbers started at O10000 to O999999. Then came OA1 to OA99999, OB1 to OB99999 and so on until OZ1 to OZ99999 in September 1957. The OC series – new copies of the original design, both in large and small versions – was reserved for Committee members. These are very rare. Then there was 1A1 to 1A99999, 2A1 to 2A99999, 3A1 to 3A99999 and so on up to 9A99999 (issued in 1959). These were followed by the B series from 1960 to 1961, the C series from 1962 to 1963, the D series from 1964 to 1965 and finally the E series from 1966 to 1967.

There is a file note that 2E1 was available in December 1967, well after the introduction of the square logo in February 1967 – and a badge with

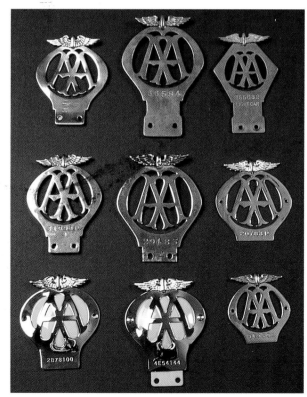

Pre-war flat badges, large and small versions, a pentagonal 'light car' type and post-war domed types.

23

a 9E number is also known to exist – so it seems that either old-style badges were still being made late in 1967 or else there was a big stockpile of them beforehand. This is quite possible, because *two million* badges were issued over the ten-year A–E series (and about another million and a half between 1945 and 1956). That means that towards the end of the period, which was one of incredible membership growth, about 50,000 badges were being issued roughly every three months – about 500 per day! This is justifiable when looking at the membership-increase figures – 1.8 million at the end of 1956, 3.7 million at the end of 1966. This is why the post-war bulged-out-front style is still very common and worth only a few pounds, despite its age.

In general terms, the allocation of serial numbers is as follows:

1 to 999999	1906–30	
A to P suffixes	1930–45	
RST suffixes	1946–56	(flat motorcycle badges)
WXYZA suffixes	1956–67	(domed motorcycle badges)
OA to OZ prefixes	1945–57	
1A to 9A prefixes	1957–9	
1B to 9B prefixes	1960–1	
1C to 9C prefixes	1962–3	
1D to 9D prefixes	1964–5	
1E to 9E prefixes	1966–7	

Types of 1967 square badges. These include oversize Committee, Relay, the AA fleet set, Advanced Driver and Maltese AA badge with reversed colours.

Jersey and Guernsey badges, with unadopted trial designs (middle row left and bottom row centre), and two AA-made retro issues of the 1945 pattern with the date stamped on at the bottom instead of a badge number (examples were also made of the 1906 and 1930 types).

It is important to note that a badge number is *not* the membership number.

The new-style square badges were introduced from February 1967 and were not numbered at all. There has been almost no variation in style or manufacture since and so they cannot be dated. The square badge was issued as a straight sale, not a hire fee.

There are, however, interesting types based on the new style. One consists of a single 'A' within a laurel-leaf surround, issued to AA members who passed the AA Advanced Driving Course in the 1970s. They are very hard to find. There is also a badge for Relay members and a version for Committee members, which has a chevron above the double 'A's – the last remnant of the old wings. There is a set of three AA staff versions for England, Scotland and Wales, having national flags surmounted by a tiny AA emblem in one top corner, which were for internal issue to AA fleet drivers only – but some have got on to the open market. Finally, a private manufacturer in Malta made an entirely unauthorised version for the Maltese AA in reversed colours – yellow 'A's on a black background.

The traditional winged badge, in both pre-war and post-war styles, was adopted by other Commonwealth Automobile Associations (set up like the United Kingdom AA), usually adding the name of the country in an oval above the wings. Variations thus exist for countries such as Malaya, New Zealand, Kenya and Rhodesia. There are similar versions for Jersey and Guernsey. A number of overseas Associations have adopted the new square design, which, like its predecessor, is arguably the most famous motoring symbol of all time, known worldwide.

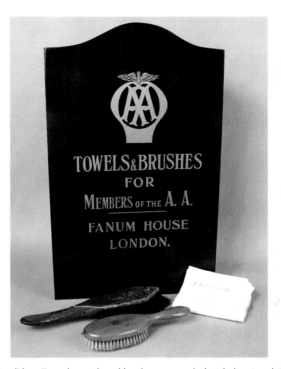

An AA 'hotel' box. Even the towels and brushes were marked with the winged AA badge.

Keys

Before the First World War, wooden cabinets containing towels and brushes were installed by the AA at country hotels for the use of members, who would get filthy driving open cars on unmade roads. The cabinets came in several designs, some with a glass oval window, but all were opened with a small steel key with a fretted, crossed 'AA' in the head.

Although telephone boxes began to appear in 1911, they were first manned by patrols and members could use the telephones only when the patrol was on duty. It was not until August 1919 that members were issued with their own keys. These had a large round head with fretted double 'A's and the legend 'The key to the open road'. Hotel box locks were changed to accept the new keys. The keys issued in 1920 were so dated and were made by H & T Vaughan of Willenhall (they were taken over by Yale & Towne in 1929). In 1921 the keys had a smaller, solid head and were dated 1921, but from then on the date was omitted and the wording 'Property of the AA' included, together with the key number. The round-head type lasted until 1947, when a hexagonal shape was introduced. By agreement with the RAC, these keys fitted RAC boxes too and vice versa.

The 1947-pattern keys, made by Yale, were stamped 'Finder will be

Keys, a pre-war key case, post-war key fobs – and a special presentation key with enamelled centre.

rewarded by the AA' because it was possible to trace the owner of any such 'lost' key from the number (although this was not the membership number). One such owner was traced from a key found in Italy.

With the introduction of the new logo in 1967, the keys were redesigned, with a square head and initially impressed logo, later embossed, and no number. The cost of recording key issues was too great when there were millions of members. The 10 millionth AA key was issued in 1966, and in 1976 a very large gold-plated key was presented to the AA Chairman to mark the issue of the 20 millionth key.

Key-related items, including a silver inkwell and the two 10-million and 20-million commemorative keys.

Ashtrays

The earliest AA ashtray dates from 1910. It has a shallow bowl covered with a thin replica of a first-pattern AA badge complete with telephone number, which enables it to be dated (because the telephone numbers changed).

Between 1910 and 1913 another version was made, with a winged badge set vertically – again with a telephone number enabling dating. This type of ashtray, without any inscription, was mass-produced in the 1920s and 1930s in slightly different variations and sizes for use by AA office staff and as presentation items. It is possible that one of these was produced to commemorate the first 100,000 members in 1920, because one was certainly produced to commemorate the first half-million in 1933 and another for the first million in 1950.

Others were produced to commemorate the first post-war AIT (*Alliance Internationale de Tourisme* – International Touring Alliance) conference in 1945 and the AA's Golden Jubilee in 1955. All are variations of a bowl with a vertical winged badge.

After the introduction of the new badge in 1967, old ashtrays continued in use but were not used for presentation. A new triangular dish in satin-finish steel came into use, having the new badge etched into the metal at one corner. In 1976 a rectangular black-glass dish, carrying the AA's armorial bearings, was issued in two sizes for use in offices and for presentation.

A selection of smoking-related artefacts. These include ashtrays, book matches, white ball match striker and a superb cigarette box from the AA boardroom.

Handbooks

The first handbook was issued in 1908. It is an extremely rare volume – only one copy is known to exist, in the AA's own historic collection (there were two, but one was stolen). They were then issued annually until the 1914/15 version, with a gap until the 1919 edition, and annually again until 1930. They became biennial for 1931/2, 1932/3, 1933/4 and so on up to the 1939/40 issue. The next was the 1949 edition (actually undated, but with calendars for 1949 and 1950). Then there was a gap until the 1951/2 issue, annual issues for 1954, 1955 and 1956, then double issues for 1957/8, 1958/9, 1959/60 and 1960/1. Annual issues came out in 1962 and 1963, then issues for two years at a time for 1964/5, 1966/7 and onwards.

Note, however, that there were two issues in 1923 – the first called the *AA and MU Handbook*, the second called the *AA Handbook 2nd Edition*. For each of the 1938/9 and 1939/40 editions, the handbooks were divided into two volumes – an 'AA Hotels Handbook' and an 'AA Garage Handbook'. (There were also a number of hotel supplements published in the 1920s and 1930s, which eventually became the restaurant and boarding-house guidebooks. There was also one in 1944.) The 1932 edition refers to 'enormous demand … necessitating the production of two editions each year' – by which was meant two *printings*. There were separate versions for Scotland in 1949/50 and 1951/2.

The 1992/3 edition is (wrongly) described as the '51st edition' – if the split hotel/garage handbooks of 1938/9 and 1939/40 are counted as two volumes both comprising one edition, then the 1992/3 edition was actually the 56th. The next issue (published in 1994) was called, again wrongly, the 52nd edition, but year dates were re-adopted for 1997/8. Then came the 1999–2000 issue. The next was marked 2001–3.

Separate Irish handbooks were issued from 1928 to 1932, then 1933/4, annually to 1939, the first post-war edition in 1947/8, then 1949/50, 1951/2, nothing in 1953, then 1954, 1955, 1956. Double years occurred from 1957/8 to 1960/1, annuals in 1961, 1962 and 1963, and doubles again from 1964/5 onwards as in the United Kingdom.

The 1909 AA Handbook. The first one of 1908 was identical except for the date

Road signs

When motorists started to travel further afield by car, warning and location signs were needed – most of which (to the 1930s) were provided by the AA. The wooden AA signs before the First World War were soon superseded by metal signs from the 1920s onwards. All sorts of warning, direction, information and safety signs were put up, the AA badge even appearing on fingerposts it erected or refurbished.

The most famous were the circular signs erected at either end of villages to indicate to motorists where they were, how far to the next village and how far from London. The first of the circular signs appeared in 1906/7, but by 1919 the more familiar ones with a central band bearing the village name had come out in yellow and dark blue and included the words 'and Motor Union' under the AA title – this wording was dropped in 1923 and the dark blue changed to black. (A variation village sign used between 1912 and 1920 was in the shape of an AA badge.) Although more than thirty thousand of the village signs were erected, very few have survived, and there are fewer than one hundred still *in situ*; the vast majority were taken down in the invasion scare of 1940 and went for scrap. A very few were just painted over, as were the telephone-box names.

Various AA signs, mounted on a hired lorry for the AA's Golden Jubilee procession in Hyde Park. A lorry had to be hired as the AA used no flatbeds at the time. The warning pole ball is hugely oversized so it could be readily seen on the parade – the originals, hoisted up poles by garage agents to warn of traps, were about the size of an apple.

Preparing temporary signs for the World Cup, 1966. Stencilled lettering was painted in by hand to give solid letters.

Triangular danger and warning signs indicated schools, crossroads, dangerous corners, level crossings and other potential hazards. There were directional signs to towns, hanging signs for hotels and garages, illuminated lantern signs for hotels, garages and AA offices, bridge nameplates, special-event notices, car-park directions and 'no racing' signs, which had interchangeable racecourse names. Practically all of these were enamelled metal signs made by Franco of London and are highly collectable. Modern AA special-event signs are made by high-tech computer processes.

Toys and models

A very large range of AA-inspired toys and models has been produced for many years, avidly sought by collectors. Numerous articles have been written in specialist magazines. There are around a dozen different types of model of patrol with motorcycle and sidecar, made by different manufacturers and in different scales (mostly in the 1950s and 1960s), a range of telephone boxes – some at OO scale for model railways, some in the form of money boxes and telephone-directory holders – pre-war road signs mounted on poles, and scores of different vehicles ranging from cheap minivan models to expensive collectors' edition hand-built vehicle transporters. Corgi models produced individual vehicles and boxed sets. Specialist dealers bought blanks and painted them as specific vehicles, such as the experimental Morris Road Service vans of the late 1930s. There is even a large-scale model of the modern AA-liveried BMW solos used in city centres. Hand-built one-offs, particularly of AA aircraft, offer further scope to collectors.

To commemorate the AA's seventy-fifth anniversary, pewter models were produced of an AA patrol by a 'loopway' (diversion) sign and of a cycle scout. The latter was made for presentation only. An addition to the genre was a range of figures by Gerry Ford, of Crown Gardens, Fleet GU51 3LT, in

Models of Road Service Outfits. The model shown top centre and the box to its left are highly detailed models made by Bassett Lowke. The central boxed set is pre-war. The two motorcycles on the left are from the 1990s.

54 mm scale, depicting various AA uniforms ranging from a cycle scout via a wartime AA Home Guard to a modern patrol, no longer in production. He also still produces a telephone box, saluting patrol and motorcycle combination inspired by the BBC television series *The Last Salute*.

Telephone boxes and figures. Apart from the two silver seventy-fifth-anniversary presentation pieces and the signs on poles, all these items are post-1980s. The figures are by Gerry Ford.

Mainly modern models, ranging from a Brava (jointly commissioned by the AA and Vauxhall) at the top, two boxed sets produced by Gerry Ford in the centre and top left, to Corgi vehicles below and top right (Corgi boxed set not shown), as well as a specialist limited-edition Relay vehicle (centre bottom) and a 1950s Land Rover with original box (centre top).

33

Uniforms

The first AA uniform was merely a black peaked cap and a yellow oilskin for bad weather. In 1912 military-style full uniforms were issued, complete with first-aid pouch on a sash and a brass arm badge. No originals of these uniforms are known to exist. In 1947 new open-neck versions were introduced (at the same time as open-neck police uniforms) and in 1955 safety helmets for patrols on motorcycles. Brass detachable collar badges were used from 1957 in place of previous woven emblems. From 1961 an army-style curved shoulder flash was worn, bearing the name of the area in which the patrol served, in yellow on a black background. There are variations for all of the United Kingdom including the Channel Islands. There were other shoulder flashes for specialist job titles such as Port Officer and Senior Frontier Officer. Superintendents had their insignia made of bullion wire, not simple embroidery. Inspectors had arm and collar badges made on a red background – a carry-over from the red first-aid-pouch sashes – and red collars on their uniforms. An AA badge was worn on the upper arm like army divisional patches. Cloth stripes were used for sergeants, army style, yellow on black, but were much smaller for the later olive drab uniforms. Buttons, in various sizes, were black composite material moulded with an AA badge. Long-service badges were also introduced, being inverted chevrons and stars on a black background – one silver chevron for five years, gold for ten years and a gold star for twenty years – which, when worn in combination, could denote any length of service in five-year intervals.

In 1969 new olive drab uniforms were issued, together with new square-logo insignia. The 1969 uniforms brought with them new rank insignia based on the police system, with 'pips' of the national emblems of England (rose), Scotland (thistle), Wales (daffodil) and Ireland (shamrock) superimposed with crossed 'A's based on the AA armorial design. Special metal collar badges were used for Inspectors and Superintendents. Square metal cap badges were used on peaked caps and on berets. Female receptionists wore a huge double 'A' badge in yellow enamel on a gold chain round their necks. In the 1990s a more practical look came into use – reflective safety jackets, green pullovers and an optional baseball cap.

Some of this insignia is available to collectors, particularly the cap badges. For some reason not understood, the unwinged

The last version of the 'old style' uniform, with arm badges, crash helmet and aerodynamic motorcycle fittings.

The olive drab uniform of 1969 being worn by Patrol Martin Green, who was awarded the Patrol Service Cross for an action risking his life while on duty. The Patrol Service Medal is awarded for courageous or outstanding initiative and devotion to duty.

brass cap badge of the early days was retained for many years, up to the introduction of the post-war uniform of 1947. Numbered and un-numbered versions exist, as well as some silver-plated versions, but these might be privately done by the patrol concerned. Winged collar badges in metal matched winged cap badges, of which there was a rare 'Stabrite' version.

There is an extremely rare cap badge with matching collar badges for the AA Voluntary Service Corps. This corps was set up in the First World War when AA members

AA allsorts. (From top) A presentation pen for the Golden Jubilee in 1955, staff membership lapel badges, Guards to Hastings commemorative plaque, various tiepins and lapel badges and 'pips' for the 1969 shoulder insignia – the central crown was for a Superintendent.

AA staff badges. VSC at the top (with a collar badge below), numbered and unnumbered wingless pattern cap badges, bullion examples and a modern square logo.

provided their cars – and chauffeurs – for service with the War Office on courier and other duties, providing the drivers with insignia to show they were on 'active duty'. The cap badge is a normal winged badge with a scroll bearing the title underneath, while the collar badge is a smaller winged badge with the letters 'VSC' underneath. A few replicas were privately made in 1999 but are much thinner than the originals and have a raised rim on the underside.

An Austin Seven van on trial, 1932. It was deemed too expensive to be taken into service.

Vehicles

Cycle scouts used their own cycles, for which they were paid an allowance, a practice that continued up to 1939. Solo motorcycles were used by inspectors from 1912 and the first combinations – known as Road Service Outfits, or RSOs for short – were issued in 1919. The early machines were Chater Leas, followed by Triumphs and then BSAs, which formed the vast majority of the AA machines right up to 1968. The mainstay machines were M20s before the Second World War and M21s afterwards.

Then followed Minivans, Maestro vans, Metros, Escorts, Bedfords, Land Rovers of all types, as well as all sorts of one-off specialist recovery vehicles. In 1994 the first of a fleet of specially designed standard-issue patrol vehicles came into service: the Vauxhall Brava, which has a unique body pod specially made for the AA (the first Brava in service is at Milestones Museum, Basingstoke). However, a patrol is just as likely to arrive in some other type of vehicle.

Quite a few RSOs survive. Every few years one seems to turn up at an automobilia sale or is advertised in the motorcycle press, and derelict examples are found in barns, while others that have been put to civilian use are restored to their AA paint scheme.

The modern Brava van. The basic vehicle is a Vauxhall, with storage pod specially made for the AA by Island Plastics on the Isle of Wight. The first one into service was preserved by the AA when time-expired and is on display at Milestones Museum, Basingstoke. This one, in service in Scotland, sports the AA Scotland fleet badge.

Further reading

The AA. *Golden Milestone.* 1955. Published by the AA to celebrate its Golden Jubilee. Many copies were printed and can still be found in second-hand bookshops.

Barty-King, Hugh. *The AA: A History of the Automobile Association 1905–1980.* AA, 1980. Published to celebrate the AA's seventy-fifth anniversary, this is the definitive history of the Association. It has 320 pages with about one thousand illustrations and a big colour section at the back picturing badges, signs, uniforms, vehicles, telephone boxes and more. It was quite expensive in its day at £15 so not many were sold. Consequently it is hard to find and will be expensive (it is no longer in print and the AA has no stock left).

Cooke, Stenson. *This Motoring.* AA, 1930. Many copies were printed and can still be found in second-hand bookshops.

Quinn, Paul. *The Yellow Motorbike.* Privately published by the author, 1982. A most entertaining read, by a former patrol, covering the last ten years when motorcycles were in service, from the day he joined until he was issued with a Minivan. Available from the author, £6.50 post free, from 32 Windsor Way, Polegate, Sussex BN26 6QD.

The end of an era, 1968. A radio, safety helmet and new-style box made this AA motorcycle the last word in a motoring assistance vehicle of the time.

Places to visit

From the 1950s the AA took steps to preserve its historical artefacts and has built up a large collection of material. The best and most interesting items are now on public show at Milestones Museum (see below). An up-to-date listing of all road-transport museums in the United Kingdom can be found on www.motormuseums.com

Avoncroft Museum of Historic Buildings, Stoke Heath, Bromsgrove, Worcestershire B60 4JR. Telephone: 01527 831363 or 831886. Website: www.avoncroft.org.uk Also houses the National Telephone Museum, which includes examples of an AA telephone box, a Road Service Centre with integral box and wind-powered generator, and all the pedestal types.

Eardisland Dovecote Trust, c/o the Secretary: Barry Freeman, Holmlea, Eardisland, near Leominster, Herefordshire HR6 9BP. Telephone: 01544 388226. The dovecote houses a small museum of rare AA material and the only known existing pre-war (1927-pattern) AA telephone box is displayed in a garden opposite.

Milestones Museum, Leisure Park, Churchill Way West, Basingstoke, Hampshire RG21 6YR. Telephone: 01256 477766. Website: www.milestones-museum.com The collection consists of vehicles (a Brava, a Minivan and the first Land Rover, as well as some typical RSOs), uniforms, telephones, models, signs, badges, cartoons and presentation items.

National Motor Museum, Beaulieu, Brockenhurst, Hampshire SO42 7ZN. Telephone: 01590 612345. Website: www.beaulieu.co.uk Has a small display of similar items to those in Milestones Museum, including a special AA 'Watch for horses' New Forest sign.

In the 1960s Road Service Centres were set up at strategic points. These were basically a hut attached to a box, where a patrol was permanently on duty. About sixty were built, but only two survive, one of which is at the National Telephone Museum at the Avoncroft Museum of Historic Buildings (see above).

Index